CRAFTY
IDEAS FROM
SCIENCE

Many thanks to Margaret Montgomery for her help
with additional projects.

Published in Great Britain in 1993 by
Exley Publications Ltd, 16 Chalk Hill,
Watford, Herts WD1 4BN, United Kingdom.

Published in the USA in 1993 by
Exley Giftbooks, 232 Madison Avenue,
Suite 1206, NY 10016, USA.

Reprinted 1994

A copy of the CIP is available from the
British Library

ISBN 1-85015-392-2

Series designer: Gillian Chapman.
Editorial: Margaret Montgomery.
Typeset by Brush Off Studios, St Albans, Herts AL3 4PH.
Printed and bound by Graficas Reunidas SA, Madrid, Spain.

CRAFTY
IDEAS FROM
SCIENCE

Myrna Daitz

Pictures
by
Gillian Chapman

EXLEY
NEW YORK • WATFORD, UK

In the same series:

Contents

Introduction

Crafty Ideas from Science contains over twenty-five projects that can be made by children between five and ten years of age. All the projects are safe and introduce children to science in a lively way.

Each project is illustrated with simple step-by-step instructions and includes science facts which explain how and why the project works. Some of the projects need adult supervision and these have been clearly marked.

There are instructions for bending light, making a rainbow, taking fingerprints, moving water, blowing bubbles and many other ideas, demonstrating magnetism, metamorphosis, friction and gravity. Everything in the book can be made using basic materials found at home or in school, so if a project doesn't work the first time, it can be tried again with no great expense involved.

While they are doing the projects, children will learn basic craft skills and will develop confidence when they see the projects work before their eyes.

Our author, Myrna Daitz, is a schoolteacher with years of experience of craft teaching. She has deliberately designed the projects to be simple and has tested them all in the classroom.

With *Crafty Ideas from Science*, children will discover that science really can be fun.

Stalactites and Stalagmites

What you need :-

Two glass jars.
Household washing soda.
Two heavy nails.
A spoon.
An empty box.
Four pieces of string.
Hot water.

Science Fact :-
Stalactites hang from the roof of a cave & stalagmites rise up from the floor.

1. Fill both jars with hot water and stir in the washing soda. Keep adding soda until no more will dissolve.

2. Twist the four pieces of string together, then tie each end to a nail. Make sure the string is long enough to reach from the bottom of one jar, over the empty box and into the bottom of the other jar. The heavy nail should keep the string secure in each jar.

3. Leave the experiment in a warm place. Soon you will see the solution soak along the string. When it reaches the box, drips will fall into it.

SCIENCE FACTS

As the water EVAPORATES from the box and the string, you will see STALACTITES and STALAGMITES forming from the SALTS that are left.

Real STALACTITES and STALAGMITES are made from calcium-salt deposits caused by water, full of calcium, constantly dripping from the ceiling of caves. The stalactites hang from the roof and the stalagmites rise up from the floor of the cave.

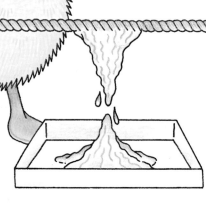

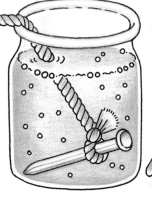

Why Do They Float?

What you need :-

A drinking glass.
Water.
Salt.
A spoon.
An egg.
A sewing needle.
A bowl.

1. Fill the glass with water and gently put the egg into it. The egg will sink immediately.

2. Remove the egg, then add lots of salt to the water, stirring it until no more will dissolve.

3. Gently put the egg back into the glass and watch it float.

★ ★ ★ ★ ★

1. Fill a bowl almost to the top with water.

2. *Very* carefully place the needle on the surface of the water. It will float.

SCIENCE FACTS

1. *The egg floats because salt water is much HEAVIER than drinking water. Heavy liquid will support things much better than light liquid. It is much easier to float in the sea than in a swimming pool.*

2. *The needle will float because water has a skin called SURFACE TENSION. The water molecules pull one another, and the ones at the surface are pulled closer than those below the surface, so they hold the needle up.*

Moving Water

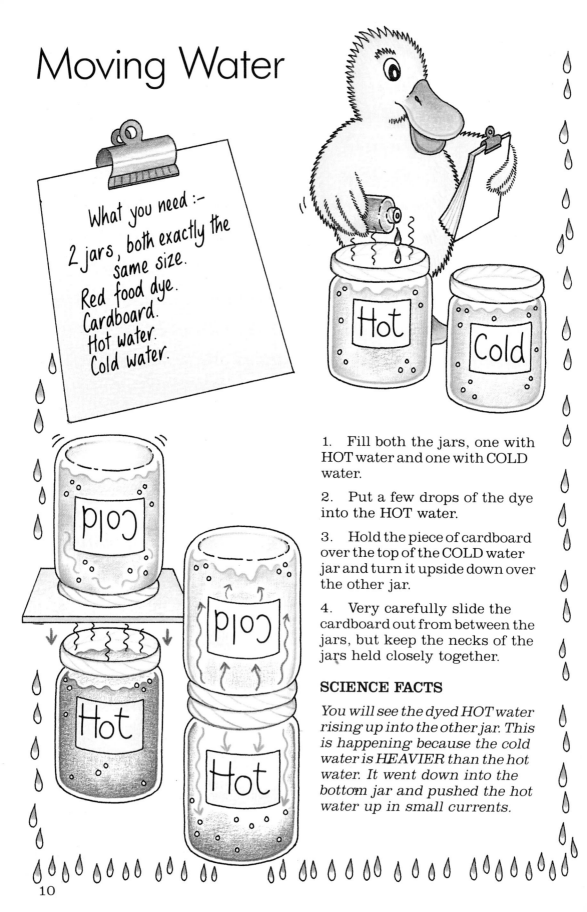

What you need :-
2 jars, both exactly the
same size.
Red food dye.
Cardboard.
Hot water.
Cold water.

1.   Fill both the jars, one with HOT water and one with COLD water.

2.   Put a few drops of the dye into the HOT water.

3.   Hold the piece of cardboard over the top of the COLD water jar and turn it upside down over the other jar.

4.   Very carefully slide the cardboard out from between the jars, but keep the necks of the jars held closely together.

SCIENCE FACTS

You will see the dyed HOT water rising up into the other jar. This is happening because the cold water is HEAVIER than the hot water. It went down into the bottom jar and pushed the hot water up in small currents.

Snowflakes

Science Fact :-
All snowflakes are six sided shapes. No two are the same !

What you need :-
Snowflakes.
A magnifying glass.
Black paper.
White crayons.
White paper doilies.
Cotton thread.

1. Examine snowflakes under a magnifying glass. Look at the many different shapes of the crystals.

2. Using white crayons, draw as many of the different shapes on black paper as you can remember. Hang them up using the thread.

3. Paste small white paper doilies on to black paper. Make a tiny hole in the top, thread cotton through, then hang the "snowflakes" from the ceiling.

SCIENCE FACTS

On a dry, clear day the water in the air is INVISIBLE. This is called VAPORIZED WATER. When the air TEMPERATURE is freezing, the VAPORIZED WATER forms CRYSTALS of ice. Snowflakes are ICE CRYSTALS. They are light and delicate.

When snow falls it seems very thick and heavy. In fact the snow is just water and there is far less of it than you may think.

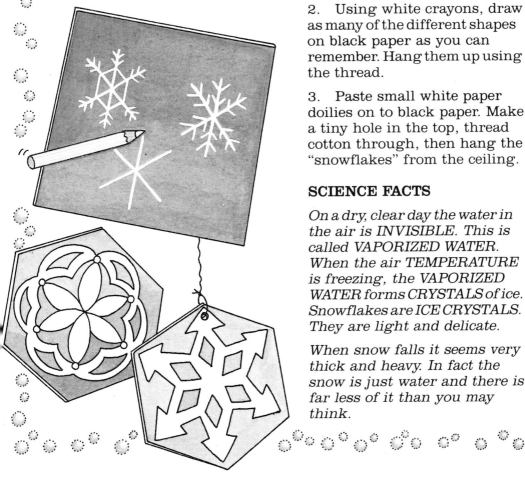

Blowing Bubbles

1. Mix the dishwashing liquid, water and glycerine together thoroughly. Let this mixture stand for several hours (the longer it stands, the stronger the bubbles).

2. Remove all the soap suds from the top of the mixture. It is now ready to use.

3. Curve one end of the wire into a small loop. Twist the end over to make a nice firm circle with a long handle.

4. Dip the wire into the bubble mixture and slowly pull it out. The circle will now have a film of soap across it. Blow the circle gently to make the soap bubbles.

What you need :-
A piece of thin wire.
Mild dishwashing liquid.
Warm water.
A few drops of glycerine.

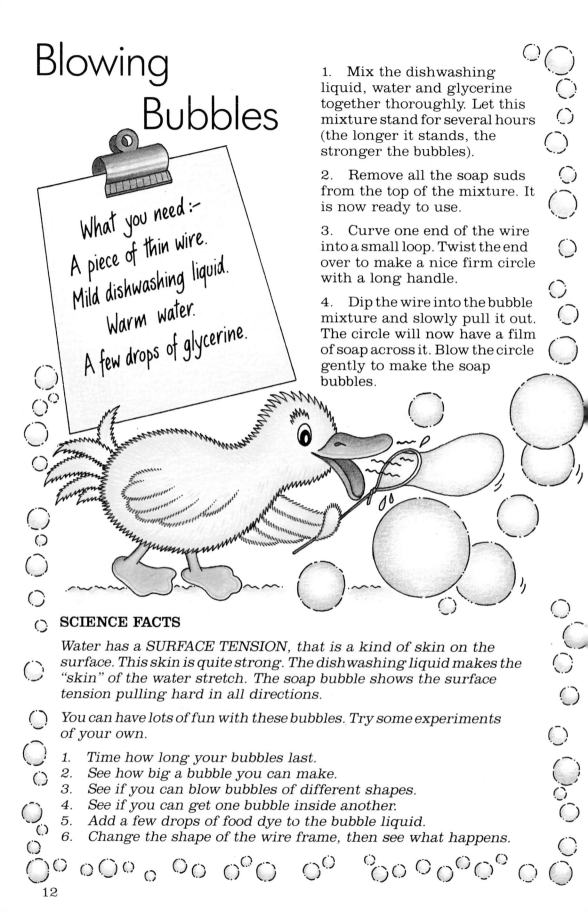

SCIENCE FACTS

Water has a SURFACE TENSION, that is a kind of skin on the surface. This skin is quite strong. The dishwashing liquid makes the "skin" of the water stretch. The soap bubble shows the surface tension pulling hard in all directions.

You can have lots of fun with these bubbles. Try some experiments of your own.

1. *Time how long your bubbles last.*
2. *See how big a bubble you can make.*
3. *See if you can blow bubbles of different shapes.*
4. *See if you can get one bubble inside another.*
5. *Add a few drops of food dye to the bubble liquid.*
6. *Change the shape of the wire frame, then see what happens.*

Making Clouds

What you need :-
A very large jar with a lid.

Water.
Chalk powder (crushed chalk).
A round balloon, with the "neck" cut off.
Scissors.
A thick rubber band.

Science Fact :-
Clouds form when air containing vaporized water cools.

1. Pour a small amount of water into the jar. Put the lid tightly on and leave it for twenty minutes.

2. Remove the lid and add some chalk powder.

3. Immediately cover the jar with the balloon, and put a rubber band around the neck of the jar to keep the balloon firmly stretched.

4. Press the balloon down with your fist to compress the air. Hold it like this for about twenty seconds. Remove the balloon and you will have made a "cloud".

SCIENCE FACTS

Clouds form when air containing VAPORIZED WATER cools. Cool air cannot hold much vaporized water so some of it CONDENSES to form clouds. When you compress the air in your jar, the air becomes warmer and ABSORBS more vaporized water. When you remove the balloon cover, the air cools and some of the vaporized water CONDENSES on the chalk dust to form a cloud.

A Rain Gauge

What you need :-

A glass jar.
A funnel - the same width as the neck of the jar.
A plant stick.
A pencil.
A ruler.

1. Using the ruler and pencil, mark one end of the plant stick at 5mm (¼″) intervals up to 10cm (4″).

2. Take the jar outside and place it in the ground, having the neck of the jar level with the top of the soil.

3. Put the funnel in the jar – and wait for it to rain.

4. When it has rained, remove the funnel and hold the measuring stick upright in the jar so it is touching the bottom. Remove the stick, make a note of the reading to the nearest 5mm (¼″), then empty the jar. If you record the rainfall every day, you can see how the amount of rain your area gets changes throughout the year.

SCIENCE FACTS

The type of plants that will grow well in your area will depend on the amount of rain and sun your area gets. Some plants need a cool, damp climate while others like a warm, dry climate.

A Barometer

Rubber band

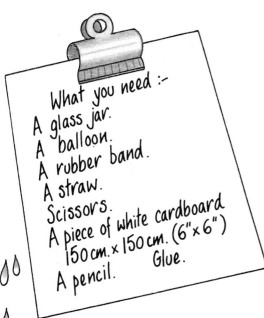

What you need :-
A glass jar.
A balloon.
A rubber band.
A straw.
Scissors.
A piece of white cardboard
150 cm. × 150 cm. (6" × 6")
Glue.
A pencil.

4. Write "Low" at the bottom and "High" at the top on the right-hand side of the cardboard. This will be the gauge.

5. Rest the cardboard against a wall or window, then position the jar, so that the free end of the straw is in front of the gauge.

1. Cut a circle out of the balloon.

2. Stretch the piece of balloon tightly over the top of the jar and hold it in place with the rubber band.

3. Glue one end of the straw to the middle of the piece of balloon. This will be the pointer.

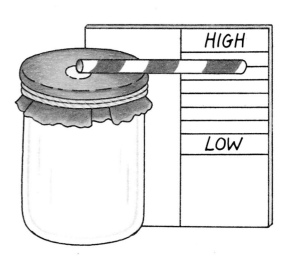

HIGH

LOW

SCIENCE FACTS

A BAROMETER measures AIR PRESSURE.

When the AIR PRESSURE around the jar RISES, it presses the piece of balloon down. This makes the pointer move up to give a HIGH reading on the gauge. When the AIR PRESSURE around the jar FALLS, the pressure inside the jar forces the piece of balloon up. This makes the pointer move down to give a LOW reading.

A drop in air pressure usually means that bad weather can be expected. A rise in air pressure usually means that better weather can be expected.

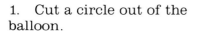

A Water Fountain

What you need :-

A small bottle with a screw top lid.
A strong plastic drinking straw.
Blu-tack.
A drawing pin (thumbtack).
Food dye.
A deep bowl or bucket of hot water.

1. ASK AN ADULT to carefully make a hole in the bottle lid.

2. Fill the bottle half-way up with cold water and add a few drops of dye.

3. Screw the lid very tightly on the bottle, then push the straw through the hole in the lid.

4. Press Blu-tack around the straw to seal up the hole in the lid.

5. Put a small piece of Blu-tack in the end of the straw and plug it with the pin.

6. Put the bottle carefully into the bowl of very hot water then remove the pin and Blu-tack from the top of the straw.

Make a hole in the bottle lid.

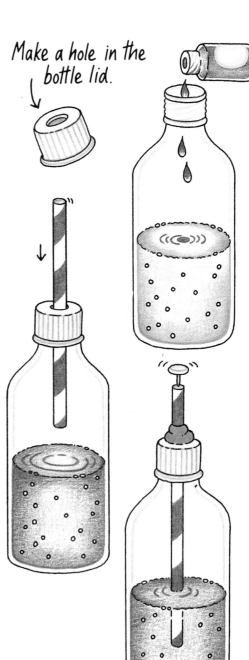

SCIENCE FACTS

The hot water will heat the air inside the bottle which will then EXPAND to force the water up through the straw. You will have a very attractive water fountain that is great fun to watch.

The Magic Glass

What you need :-
A drinking glass.
Water.
A piece of cardboard.

1. Fill the glass to the very top with water.

2. Slide the cardboard over the glass and press it firmly on.

3. Holding the glass with one hand and the cardboard with the other, very carefully turn the glass upside down.

4. Slowly let go of the cardboard.

5. The cardboard will appear to hold the water in the glass.

SCIENCE FACTS

The water will stay inside the glass because the AIR under the glass is pressing against the cardboard with more pressure than the WATER is pressing against the cardboard. AIR PRESSURE is very strong.

Science Fact :-
Air pressure is very strong.
It's MAGIC!

Water Music

1. Wash and dry the eight bottles.

2. Fill all the bottles with water, putting a different amount of water into each one.

3. Gently tap each bottle with a wooden spoon.

What you need :-
Eight glass bottles, all the same size.
A wooden spoon.
Water.

Science Fact :- Every bottle makes a different note!

SCIENCE FACTS

You will notice that every bottle makes a different note. When you get to know each note, try playing simple tunes on the musical bottles. Sound is produced by vibration. As each level of water is different, then different sounds are made when the bottles vibrate. With the different sounds you can make music. High notes are produced by the bottles with the small amounts of water in them, and low notes are produced by the bottles that have larger amounts of water in them.

The note that any object produces will depend on how many times it vibrates each second.

Watching Plants Grow

1. Soak a piece of blotting paper with water and place it on a saucer. Sprinkle mustard and cress seeds on it. Keep the paper damp and see how quickly the seeds grow. After a few days, they can be eaten in sandwiches.

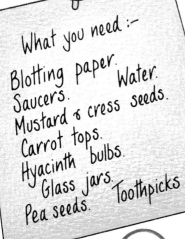

What you need :-

Blotting paper.
Saucers.   Water.
Mustard & cress seeds.
Carrot tops.
Hyacinth bulbs.
    Glass jars.   Toothpicks
Pea seeds.

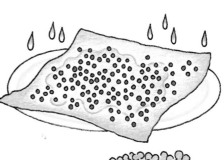

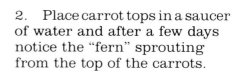

Science Fact :-
Water is needed to make ALL things grow!

2. Place carrot tops in a saucer of water and after a few days notice the "fern" sprouting from the top of the carrots.

3. Hyacinth bulbs can be grown in water in wide-necked bottles or jars. You can then see the whole growth of leaves, roots and flower. Press toothpicks into the bulb so that it can balance on the neck of the jar. The base of the bulb should just touch the water.

4. Soak the pea seeds in warm water for three hours. Line a jar with blotting paper and add water to about one-third of the way up. Put the soaked peas between the glass and the paper. Leave the jar in a warm, light place. Keep the blotting paper damp.

SCIENCE FACTS

Water is needed to make all things grow. Plants draw water up through their roots, stem and leaves.

If you turn the pea seeds upside down, they will soon turn themselves the right way so that their roots point downward. This is because in soil, roots will always grow downward to find water and food, and shoots will always grow up to the light.

Busy Worms

THIN LAYER of SILVER SAND

LAYER of DARK SOIL

What you need :—
A small goldfish bowl.
White paper.
String.
Scissors.
Soil.
Sand (silver sand is best).
Earthworms.
Leaves.

1. Put a layer of dark soil into a clean goldfish bowl. On top of the dark soil, put a thin layer of silver sand. Top this with another layer of dark soil. Continue in this way until the bowl is two-thirds full. Put the leaves on the top. Leave a large empty space between the top layer and the paper lid.

2. For the lid, cut out a circle of paper 7cm (3″) bigger than the top of the bowl. Cut out lots of tiny air holes.

Remember to water the WORMERY every day through the air holes !

3. Carefully place the worms in the bowl. Put the paper lid on, bend down the surplus paper then tie the string firmly around it. You now have an excellent wormery. Water the soil each day through the air holes.

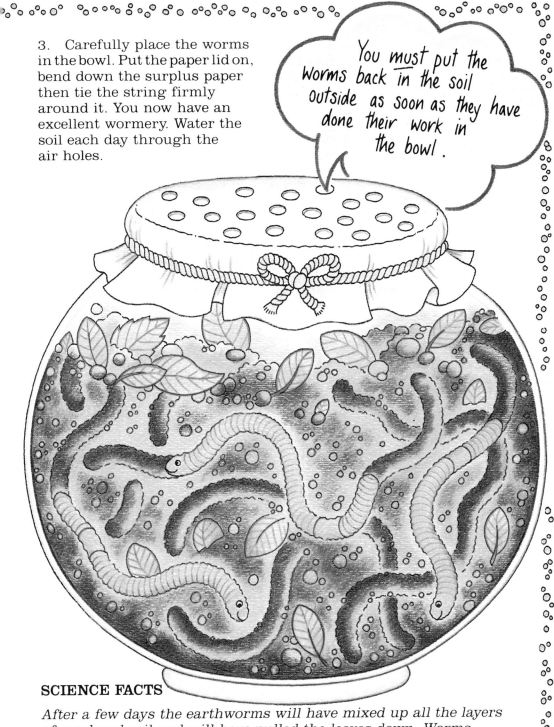

You *must* put the worms back <u>in</u> the soil outside as soon as they have done their work in the bowl.

SCIENCE FACTS

After a few days the earthworms will have mixed up all the layers of sand and soil and will have pulled the leaves down. Worms BURROW through soil and this action mixes together the HUMUS from the surface with the soil underneath. This provides air for the roots of plants. Worms are very valuable creatures and you MUST return them to their natural environment. <u>DO NOT LEAVE THEM IN THE BOWL TO DIE</u>.

Metamorphosis

What you need :-

A very large plastic jar.
A small jar of water.
A plant pot.
A cotton ball.
Soil.
A large leafy twig with butterflies' eggs or caterpillars on it.

Science Fact :-

It is very exciting to watch the gradual change from egg to caterpillar to chrysalis or then to butterfly.

1. ASK AN ADULT to make lots of small air holes in the lid of the large jar.

2. Fill the plant pot with soil then press the jar of water into the middle of the plant pot.

3. Stand the twig with the caterpillars on it in the jar of water. Plug the top of the jar with the cotton ball, so that the caterpillars will not fall into the water.

4. Carefully stand the plant pot in the plastic jar.

5. Put the lid on tightly.

SCIENCE FACTS

This experiment has to be done when there are lots of butterflies' eggs about. These are to be found on the undersides of leaves (look under cabbage leaves and nettle leaves). When all the eggs have hatched, keep putting fresh leaves of the same kind into the jar and remove the old ones. Soon you will see the caterpillars suspended from silk cord and changing into a CHRYSALIS. As soon as they change into butterflies, you MUST release them.

It is very exciting to watch the gradual change from egg to caterpillar to chrysalis and then to butterfly.

A process of change like this is called METAMORPHOSIS.

A Soil Filter

This project can be messy — put lots of newspaper down first!

What you need :-
A glass jar with a lid.
A trowel.
Soil.
Newspapers.
Water.

1. Using the trowel, half fill the jar with soil that you have collected from several different places.

2. Fill the jar to the top with water.

3. Screw the lid tightly on to the jar, then shake the jar very well. Leave the jar to stand for an hour to allow the soil to settle.

SCIENCE FACTS

When the soil mixture settles, it will have separated itself into layers. You will then be able to see the various particles that the soil is made up of. There are many different kinds of soil, and these will contain different sized particles. In your soil filter you will see gravel, peat, clay and sand. Clay soils are heavy, sandy soils are light.

Dancing Mothballs

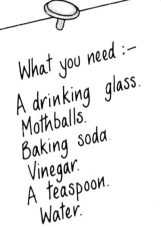

What you need :-

A drinking glass.
Mothballs.
Baking soda.
Vinegar.
A teaspoon.
Water.

1. Fill the glass almost to the top with water.

2. Add four teaspoons of baking soda and stir well until it is completely dissolved.

3. Add four teaspoons of vinegar to the mixture and stir well.

4. Carefully put four mothballs into the mixture and watch carefully.

Science Fact :-
It is fun to watch the mothballs dancing up and down.

SCIENCE FACTS

Very soon you will see bubbles of gas forming on the mothballs and this will make them float to the surface. Some of the bubbles will burst when they reach the top. Then you will see the mothballs sink slowly.

The vinegar and the baking soda when mixed together produce CARBON DIOXIDE. Bubbles of this gas stick to the rough surface of the mothballs and act as floats.

This can continue for some time before the chemicals are used up. It is fun to watch the mothballs dancing up and down.

Plaster Casts of Footprints

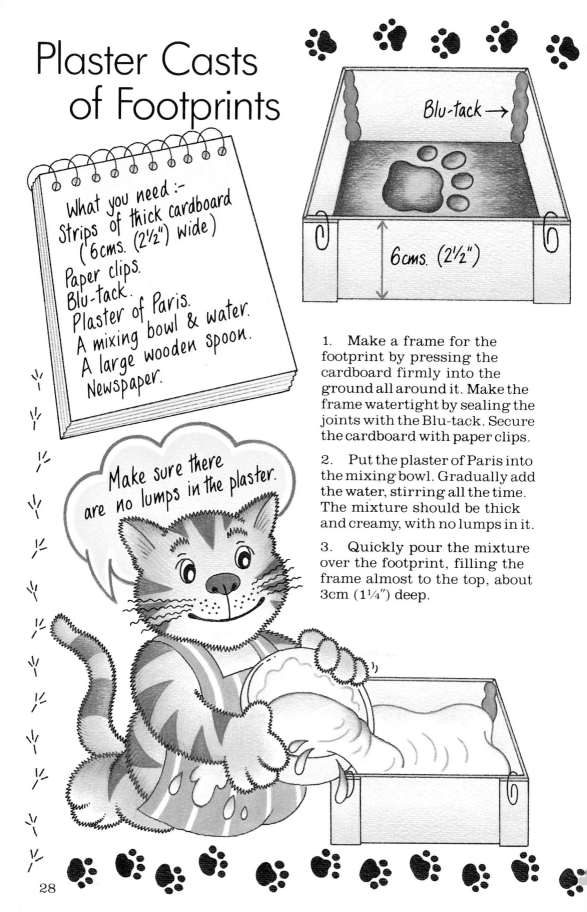

What you need :-
Strips of thick cardboard (6cms. (2½") wide)
Paper clips.
Blu-tack.
Plaster of Paris.
A mixing bowl & water.
A large wooden spoon.
Newspaper.

Blu-tack →

6cms. (2½")

Make sure there are no lumps in the plaster.

1. Make a frame for the footprint by pressing the cardboard firmly into the ground all around it. Make the frame watertight by sealing the joints with the Blu-tack. Secure the cardboard with paper clips.

2. Put the plaster of Paris into the mixing bowl. Gradually add the water, stirring all the time. The mixture should be thick and creamy, with no lumps in it.

3. Quickly pour the mixture over the footprint, filling the frame almost to the top, about 3cm (1¼") deep.

4. Cover the frame with newspaper and leave it to harden for two hours.

5. When it has set hard, remove the plaster cast. You should now have a clear cast of the footprint. Clean any soil off the cast with running water and a soft brush.

SCIENCE FACTS

Police scientists make plaster casts of footprints to help them to solve crimes. It is very interesting to make plaster casts of animal tracks. Look for the tracks near hedges and ditches. When you have made the casts, identify them from a book and record the details.

Can you identify the animal tracks shown on this page?

1.

2.

3.

4.

5.

Animal tracks:
1. Duck
2. Snake.
3. Dog
4. Bird.
5. Cat.

Taking Fingerprints

What you need :-
A very soft lead pencil.
White paper.
Adhesive tape.
A magnifying glass.

Science Fact :-
No two people have the same finger prints. This fact greatly helps the police to identify people.

1. Using the pencil, scribble quite thickly on the white paper.

2. Rub your finger all over the scribble, making it very smudgy.

3. When your finger is very black, firmly press it on to the sticky side of a piece of adhesive tape. Do this very carefully then you will see the ridges of your fingerprint.

4. Carefully turn the adhesive tape over and stick it on to a piece of white paper.

SCIENCE FACTS

The skin on fingers forms a series of ridges. Make a book of fingerprints of friends and family, marking the name of the person underneath each print. If you study the prints under a magnifying glass you will see that every one is different. No two people have the same fingerprints. This science fact greatly helps the police to identify people.

Static Electricity

What you need :-

Balloons.
Cotton thread.
A woollen sweater.
A plastic spoon.
A saucer.
Puffed rice breakfast cereal.

1. ASK AN ADULT to blow up some balloons and to tie them with thread. Rub the balloons gently for thirty seconds on a woollen sweater. Quickly put the balloons on to the nearest wall or ceiling. The balloons will cling to it.

2. Rub a plastic spoon on a woollen sweater for thirty seconds. Hold the spoon over a saucer of puffed rice. Watch the tiny puffs of rice jump up and cling to the spoon and then jump about wildly.

SCIENCE FACTS

These experiments show STATIC ELECTRICITY. A light uses electricity, but this is a different kind of electricity. The balloons stick to the walls because of the ELECTROSTATIC charge that builds up on the balloons when you rub them on the wool. It also attracts the puffs of rice to the spoon.

A Magnetic Boat Race

What you need :-
Horseshoe magnets.
Corks.   Paperclips.
Small plant sticks.
A plastic tray.   Pins.
Water.
Shiny paper.   Books.
Adhesive tape.

1.   Undo one end of a paper clip and push it into the side of a cork. The paper clip forms the metal base of the boat.

2.   Push a pin into the other side of the cork.

3.   Cut the shiny paper into triangles and, using adhesive tape, attach them, like sails, to the pins in the corks.

4.   Fix a magnet to one end of a plant stick with adhesive tape.

5. Balance the tray on two piles of books, each pile supporting the edge of the tray. Make sure the tray is level.

6. Fill the tray with water and float the boats.

7. Each player in the race holds a magnet stick under the tray to move a boat across the water. Take turns and have fun watching the boats follow your magnet.

This Magnetic Boat Race is great fun !

SCIENCE FACTS

The magnetism will pass through the plastic and the water. Magnets are now made out of a mixture of metals and minerals. Magnets attract materials with iron in them. Steel, cobalt and nickel are attracted. Brass and lead are not attracted to magnets.

Magnets have two ends. One is called the NORTH POLE and the other is the SOUTH POLE. The north pole of one magnet ATTRACTS the south pole of the other. Two north poles or two south poles REPEL one another.

Kicking A Football

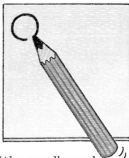

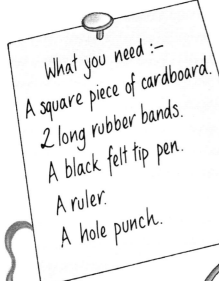

What you need :-
A square piece of cardboard.
2 long rubber bands.
A black felt tip pen.
A ruler.
A hole punch.

1. On one side of the cardboard draw a person whose leg is in a kicking position.

2. Turn the cardboard over, bottom to top, and draw a football on the left-hand side of the cardboard.

3. Using the ruler, make a mark on each side of the cardboard *exactly* in the middle between the top and the bottom. Punch a hole in each mark.

4. Thread a very long rubber band through each hole.

5. Wind up the cardboard from the bottom over to the top until the rubber bands are really tight, then pull sharply, with both hands, to loosen them. The cardboard will spin very fast.

SCIENCE FACTS

The RETINA in your eye keeps the image of an object for a moment after light is removed. You can test this by staring at a light for a few seconds then turning the light off. You will still be able to see the "image" of the light. This is called PERSISTENCE OF VISION.

When your cardboard spins very fast, it will look as if the person is moving to kick the football. This happens because the cardboard spins so fast that you have PERSISTENCE OF VISION.

A Magnifying Glass

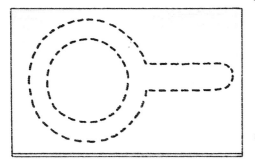

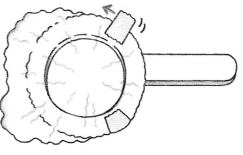

What you need :-
Stiff cardboard.
Pencil.   Water.
Scissors.
A polythene bag.
Adhesive tape.

Science Fact :-
Water acts as a magnifier for this experiment.

1. Draw the shape of a magnifying glass on the cardboard.

2. Cut around the outline and then cut out a circle from the middle.

3. Cut a piece of polythene to fit the hole in the middle.

4. Carefully stretch the polythene tightly over the hole and secure it with adhesive tape.

5. Put a drop of water on to the polythene and hold the lens over a page in a book. You will see that you have made a magnifying glass.

SCIENCE FACTS

WATER acts as a magnifier for this experiment.
A LENS can be any clear substance that has a definite shape and will bend light rays as they pass through it.
Glass, plastic and liquids can bend light. This is called REFRACTION. When you look at objects through these materials they look different.
A MICROSCOPE is an instrument that is used for looking at very small objects. It has LENSES that are a special shape. A CONVEX lens makes objects look bigger. A CONCAVE lens makes objects look smaller.

A Kaleidoscope

Science Fact :–
The mirrors and REFLECTED light produce all the interesting shapes.

What you need :–
3 rectangular handbag mirrors, all exactly the same size.
Waxed cooking paper.
Plastic food wrap.
Adhesive tape.
Scissors.
Lots of tiny pieces of bright shiny paper.

1. Lay the three mirrors face down, next to each other, on a table.

2. Using small pieces of adhesive tape, secure all three mirrors together.

3   Turn them over and bend them gently together to make a triangle, having all the mirrors *inside* the triangle. Use adhesive tape to hold the mirrors securely together in this shape.

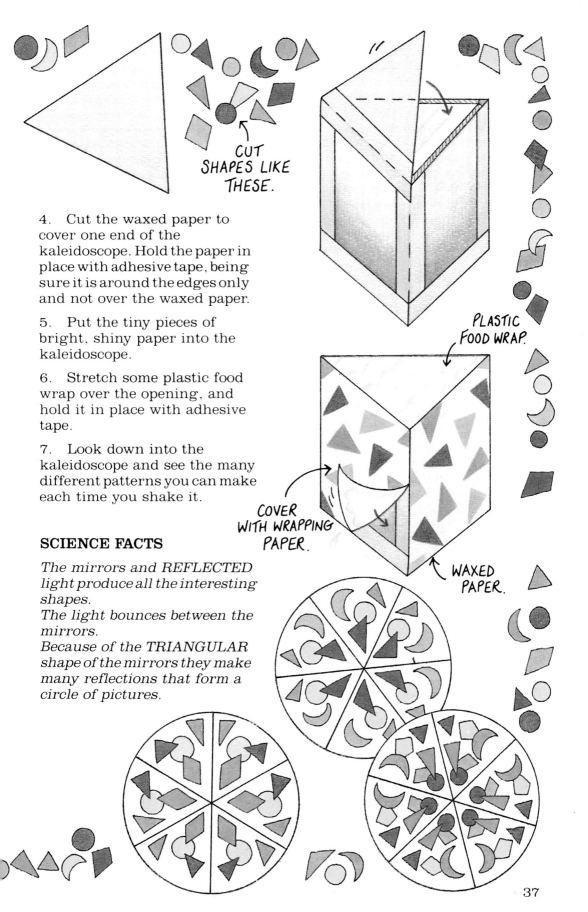

CUT SHAPES LIKE THESE.

4. Cut the waxed paper to cover one end of the kaleidoscope. Hold the paper in place with adhesive tape, being sure it is around the edges only and not over the waxed paper.

5. Put the tiny pieces of bright, shiny paper into the kaleidoscope.

6. Stretch some plastic food wrap over the opening, and hold it in place with adhesive tape.

7. Look down into the kaleidoscope and see the many different patterns you can make each time you shake it.

SCIENCE FACTS

The mirrors and REFLECTED light produce all the interesting shapes.
The light bounces between the mirrors.
Because of the TRIANGULAR shape of the mirrors they make many reflections that form a circle of pictures.

PLASTIC FOOD WRAP.

COVER WITH WRAPPING PAPER.

WAXED PAPER.

Bending Light

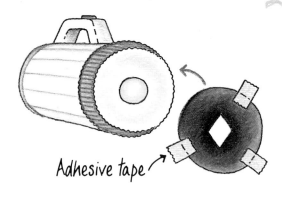

Adhesive tape

What you need :–
A hand lamp.
Scissors.
Black paper.
Adhesive tape.
A mirror.
A darkened room.

1. Cut the black paper just big enough to cover the bulb end of the lamp. Cut a slit in the middle of the paper then place it over the lamp.

2. In the dark room, switch the lamp on and point it at the mirror.

Science Fact :–
LIGHT travels in straight lines but it can be REFLECTED from objects.

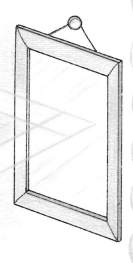

SCIENCE FACTS

You will see that the beam of light will be REFLECTED to make it shine on the wall opposite the mirror. Light travels in straight lines, but it can be REFLECTED from objects.

The light of the sun travels in a straight line to the moon, then the moon reflects it in a straight line to the earth. That is why we can see the moon at night.

Making A Rainbow

What you need :-
A glass bowl.
Water.
A small mirror.
White paper.

1. Fill the bowl with water and put it in a sunny place.

2. Put a mirror inside the bowl so that the sun can shine on it.

3. Hold up a sheet of white paper so that the sun shining on the mirror reflects onto the paper.

Science Fact :- If you hold the paper very still you will see a rainbow!

SCIENCE FACTS

If you hold the paper very still you will see a rainbow. The water in the glass acts as a PRISM. Prisms bend light. White light is made up of all the different shades of a rainbow. The prism bends these by different amounts and separates them out so that we can see them. When sunlight goes through a water drop it is split up into red, orange, yellow, green, blue, indigo and violet. You see a rainbow when the sun shines on lots of drops of water. The correct name for a rainbow is a SPECTRUM.

A Rainbow Spinner

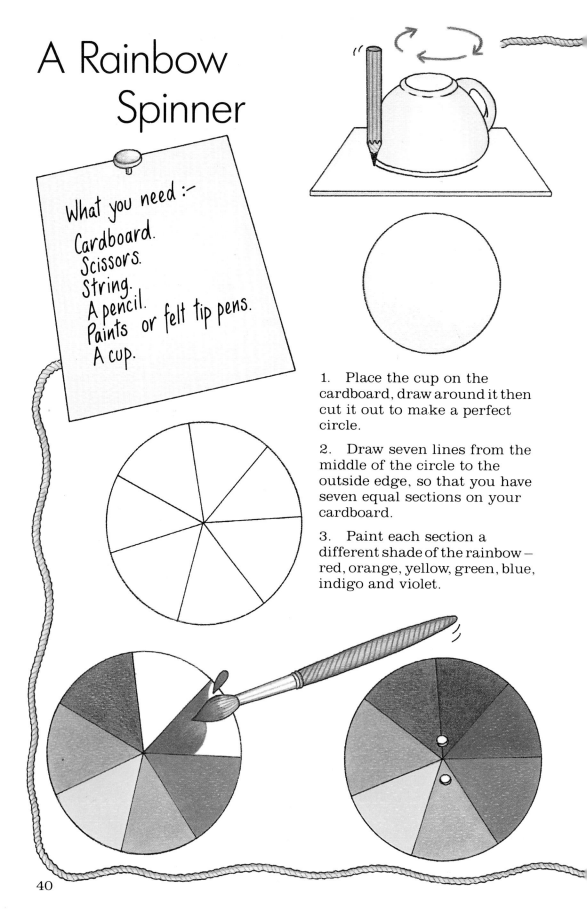

What you need :-
Cardboard.
Scissors.
String.
A pencil.
Paints or felt tip pens.
A cup.

1.   Place the cup on the cardboard, draw around it then cut it out to make a perfect circle.

2.   Draw seven lines from the middle of the circle to the outside edge, so that you have seven equal sections on your cardboard.

3.   Paint each section a different shade of the rainbow – red, orange, yellow, green, blue, indigo and violet.

4. Make two holes in the middle of the card 1cm (¼″) apart. Thread your string through one hole and then back again through the other. Tie the ends in a knot. You now have a long loop at each side of your circle.

5. Put a finger through the end of each loop. Flip the circle over the string several times until the string is well twisted.

6. Pull your hands apart and then let the string go slack. This will make your spinner go around very quickly.

Science Fact:- The rainbow spinner will look completely white!

SCIENCE FACTS

You will see the seven different shades disappear when the spinner goes very fast — it will look completely white.

Just as a rainbow is formed by raindrops splitting up white sunlight into separate bands, so you can make white light by mixing all the different shades of the rainbow together.

A Hovercraft

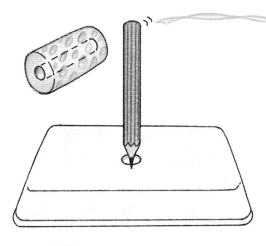

What you need :-
A lightweight food tray.
A balloon.
A cork.
Glue.
Blu-tack.
A pencil.

1.   ASK AN ADULT to make a hole right through the middle of the cork.

2.   Using the pencil, make a small hole in the middle of the food tray.

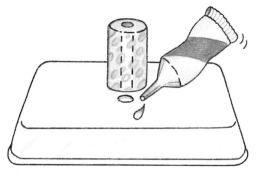

3.   Glue the cork to the underside of the food tray, being sure the holes are in line. Seal around the bottom of the cork with Blu-tack so that air cannot escape.

Make sure the bottom of the cork is sealed.

BLU-TACK.

4. Stand the food tray on a flat surface.

5. Blow up the balloon then hold the end tightly to stop the air escaping.

6. Fit the end of the balloon over the cork and gently push the food tray.

This hovercraft glides along on a cushion of air — it's just like a real hovercraft!!

SCIENCE FACTS

The air from the balloon rushes out through the hole in the cork. It forms a cushion of air which reduces the FRICTION and lifts the tray off the flat surface so that it can glide easily. This is the way a hovercraft works.

FRICTION is produced when two surfaces rub together. It acts like a brake and makes moving difficult.

Rough surfaces produce more friction than smooth surfaces.

A Snake Spiral

What you need :-
A piece of paper.
Scissors.
A pencil.
Needle & thread.
Felt tip pens or crayons.

1. Draw a spiral on the piece of paper and decorate it to look like a snake.

2. Carefully cut around the spiral.

3. To hang the snake, cut a length of yarn and thread the needle with it. Push the needle through the "head" of the snake, remove the needle and make a knot underneath the "head" so the yarn doesn't pull through.

4. Hang the snake above a radiator. As the warm air rises, the snake will start to spin.

WARM RADIATOR

SCIENCE FACTS

Warm air is LIGHTER than cold air. As air gets warm, it RISES, and is replaced with cold air. This makes AIR CURRENTS which move around indoors and outdoors.

A Submarine

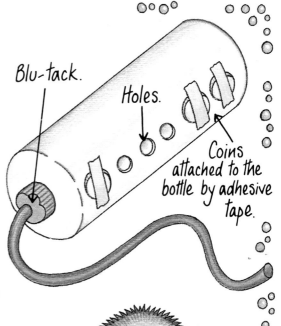

Blu-tack.

Holes.

Coins attached to the bottle by adhesive tape.

What you need :-

An empty plastic dishwashing liquid bottle.
A piece of plastic tube.
Blu-tack.
Adhesive tape.   Coins.
Scissors.
A large bowl.

1. Carefully cut three small holes in one side of the plastic bottle.

2. Using adhesive tape, fix three small coins on to the same side of the bottle.

3. Put the piece of plastic tube on to the nozzle of the bottle and seal around it with Blu-tack.

4. Fill the bowl with water, then lower the submarine into it so it fills up with water.

5. Blow through the tube. As you force air into the submarine, water will be pushed out of the holes at the bottom. As you blow more air into the submarine, it will start to rise.

SCIENCE FACTS

Air is LIGHTER than water, so when the submarine is filled with air, it becomes LIGHTER than the water and rises to the surface.
By changing the amount of air in the submarine, it will rise and sink accordingly.

A Balancing Clown

BACK of CLOWN.

Tape coins to hands

What you need :-
Thin white cardboard.
Scissors.
Glue.
Adhesive tape.
Felt tip pens or crayons.
A pencil.
2 coins of the same value.

1. Draw two clown shapes on to the cardboard and cut them out. These will be the front and back of the clown.

2. Use felt tip pens or crayons to give your clown a costume.

3. Using adhesive tape, stick one coin on to the back of each hand.

4. Glue the two halves of the clown together and leave to dry.

5. Stand the clown on its nose on the rim of a glass or on your finger and watch how it balances.

Science Fact :-

All objects have a Balancing Point. This is where the force of gravity keeps the object in balance.

Use this shape as a template to make your clown.

Balancing Point.

Position of coins

SCIENCE FACTS

All objects have a BALANCING POINT. This is where the force of GRAVITY keeps the object in balance.

The clown balances on its nose because the weight of the coins attached to the clown's hands keeps the BALANCING POINT below its nose.